TOMB RAIDERS

Discovering Tutankhamen

Simon Cheshire

Illustrated by Jim Eldridge

PACIFIC
LEARNING

© 2004 **Pacific Learning**
© 2003 Written by **Simon Cheshire**
Illustrated by **Jim Eldridge c/o Linda Rogers Associates**
Photography: Cover photo by Amos Nachoum/Corbis Uk Ltd.;
p. 4 Robert Holmes/Corbis UK Ltd.; pp. 4–5 Corel; p. 5 Dean
Conger/Corbis UK Ltd.; p. 9 Bettmann/Corbis UK Ltd.; p. 20
Bettmann/Corbis UK Ltd.; p. 23 Vanni Archive/Corbis UK Ltd.;
p. 24 Stapleton Collection/Corbis UK Ltd.; p. 25 Peter Clayton;
p. 11 Mary Evans Picture Library; p. 17 H. Burton/Griffith
Institute; p. 19 Peter Clayton; p. 50 H. Burton/Griffith
Institute; p. 54 Fulvio Roiter/Corbis UK Ltd.; p. 57 Gianni
Dagli Orti/Corbis UK Ltd.; p. 58 AKG – London; p. 60 Roger
Wood/Corbis UK Ltd.; p. 62 Neil Beer/Corbis UK Ltd.;
pp. 62–63 Corel; p. 63 Griffith Institute.
U.S. edit by **Alison Auch**

This Americanized Edition of *Tomb Raiders*, originally
published in England in 2003, is published by arrangement
with Oxford University Press.

08 07 06 05 04
10 9 8 7 6 5 4 3 2 1

Published by
Pacific Learning
P.O. Box 2723
Huntington Beach, CA 92647-0723
www.pacificlearning.com

ISBN: 1-59055-425-6
PL-7516

Printed in China.

Introduction

For many years, intrepid explorers and fortune-hunters scoured Egypt for ancient treasures. They knew that the pharaohs, who were the rulers at one time in ancient Egypt, had been buried with fabulous riches all around them.

The Egyptians believed that their pharaohs would need possessions in the **afterlife**, so along with useful items, they were buried with their riches. The ancient Egyptians also believed that pharaohs would need their body in the afterlife so they **mummified** their dead rulers, and left food and drink in their tomb. They were

Valley of the Kings, Egypt

then ready for their journey beyond death and into the afterlife.

The precious items sealed up in the tombs attracted robbers. Many tombs were broken open and stripped clean only a few years after they were sealed. Others were plundered in more recent times. When archeologists came to study ancient Egypt at the beginning of the twentieth century, they found relatively little was left. No tomb had ever been found complete and undisturbed. That was, until November 1922...

A guide stands by an ancient **sarcophagus**

The Waterboy

The waterboy scurried across the rubble. He was only nine or ten years old, but he was the most important person on the whole site. There was no doubt about it. The very sight of him brought relief to all, for without a waterboy like him, the workers could die of thirst. Oh, yes, he was the main man around here, that was for sure.

"You! Waterboy! Here! Now!"

"Yes, sir!" cried the waterboy. He scurried faster. The workers wanted a drink, and he couldn't keep them waiting. "Yes, sir, coming, yes, sir!"

The ground beneath his thin sandals was rocky and uneven. More than once he nearly stumbled.

The entire valley was like that – strewn with rocky fragments that kicked up choking clouds of dust as feet trudged across them. The Valley of the Kings, the Europeans called it. "The Valley of Heat and Flies is more like it," the waterboy thought. Although it was only a few miles from the banks of the Nile, the valley could have been a million years from anywhere. It was surrounded by high hills, and from the startlingly blue sky shone a merciless and unblinking sun.

The sun baked the rocks, and the rocks were dug up and carried away by the workers, local men hired by Mr. Carter. All over the valley, the entrance to ancient tombs had been excavated, and now the waterboy was supposed to be helping to unearth another – maybe. No one was sure anymore. They hadn't found anything for months now.

He looked over at Mr. Carter, who was sitting on a rock, by himself. He liked Mr. Carter. He treated his workers well,

Howard Carter

and he spoke the local language, unlike most of the archeologists who came here searching for tombs. Carter was a tall man, dressed in an expensive but dusty suit, with a hat firmly on his head to guard against the sun, and a thick black mustache drooping around his mouth. Although he couldn't explain why, the waterboy couldn't help feeling that Mr. Carter looked sad and nervous that day.

9

Howard Carter gave the waterboy a brief smile and a nod, and the waterboy wandered off to do some digging of his own for a while.

The waterboy had been right. Carter was indeed feeling depressed. For years, the experts in London had been saying that the Valley of the Kings had been emptied. There were no more tombs to be discovered. There was no more treasure to be uncovered. There was nothing left to be learned.

Still, Carter was convinced that the experts were absolutely wrong. He was determined to sweep the valley from one end to the other. He was certain – beyond a shadow of a doubt – that the tomb of the boy pharaoh was here somewhere. The young king, who had died mysteriously all those thousands of years ago was buried somewhere beneath the valley floor. Forget what the experts said. Carter had a nose for this kind of work and...

...Nothing had been found. Carter watched his men gouging at the rocky soil. They didn't know what he knew – that this was his last chance. If nothing was found soon, then digging would cease for good. The money and the patience of Carter's wealthy patron, Lord Carnarvon, were at an end. Carter had to make discoveries now, or he'd never get the chance to search again.

CHAPTER

2

Sixteen Steps

The only sounds, echoing against the stone cliffs, came from the digging of the workers: chipping, shoveling, scraping, clearing.

As Carter watched and worried, the waterboy idly scratched at the soil. The rubble felt sharp and hot beneath his hands. His palms were thick with dust. He crouched, sweeping aside the dirt, uncovering more dirt beneath. He brushed away more dirt, revealing yet more. Then his hand touched something hard.

Something flat.

The waterboy swept faster, ignoring the sharpness of the stones. He had found something, all right – something wide, and flat, and made of stone.

He looked up, shielding his eyes from the relentless glare of the sun. "Mr. Carter!" he yelled. "Mr. Carter!"

Carter jumped to his feet and ran over. The sound of voices started to fill the air. Workers stopped digging and looked toward the waterboy, who was beckoning wildly for people to come over and see what he had unearthed.

"He probably found a **potsherd**," they mumbled to themselves.

The waterboy dug at the earth with his hands. His fingers were raw. He could feel his heart pounding against his chest. Only minutes before, he'd been feeling that the search was pointless, but now... anything could happen.

Howard Carter joined him and quickly crouched down. "It could be the top of a larger structure," said Carter breathlessly, as he brushed sand aside in a frenzy.

It was a step.

There was a flat surface, so smooth it must have been made by human hands. Along one edge, the stone turned down, into the ground.

Carter immediately ordered the workers to dig there. The waterboy stood back. Dozens of shovels were aimed at the area in front of the step. Dazzling sunlight threw twisting shadows on the ground as they worked. Anticipation hung in the air. However tired they were feeling, they dug as quickly as they could. This could be a find. This could mean bonus payments for all of them!

Soon, a second step had been cleared.

It was undeniable. These were steps leading underground.

Carter could hardly contain his excitement. He tried to calm himself down. "Don't get your hopes up yet," he told himself. It might be nothing. "It might be nothing of importance."

Then he allowed himself to think the unthinkable. It might be the one tomb he had spent years looking for.

As fast as the heat of the day would allow, the workers dug. Empty buckets were filled and emptied and filled again as the hole in the ground grew steadily.

One step after another was revealed, until there were sixteen.

Below ground level, at the foot of the staircase, was a large plaster block, taller than a person. Across its rough surface were what appeared to be... markings?

Carter took a closer look, examining the markings on the block. They were the imprints of the ancient Egyptian **hieroglyphics**. Great age and the rough material of the plaster combined to make the hieroglyphs nearly impossible to see.

Yet they were clearly there. This was an ancient hiding place of some kind, that much was certain.

The workers and the waterboy stood jostling each other at the top of the stone steps. They spoke together hurriedly, in hushed voices, about the possibilities of discovery and the danger that could result from disturbing the resting places of the dead. The waterboy flicked his hair from his eyes with a grimy hand. Talk of disturbing the dead worried him, but the

workers seemed willing to brush it off. Their thoughts were on their bonuses. This was undoubtedly going to be a red-letter day for them too – not just for Carter.

Carter took off his hat and fanned his face for a moment or two. Flies buzzed around his head and he impatiently swatted them away.

Now was a time for clear, careful thought. He couldn't afford to make a single mistake. The proper thing to do would be to summon Lord Carnarvon to the site and tell him of the find. Carter dashed back up the steps.

CHAPTER 3

The Boy King

Lord Carnarvon

Lord Carnarvon was not a young man. His wealth normally gave him a comfortable life, but nothing could protect him from the scorching temperatures of the Egyptian desert.

"This had better be worth it, Carter, m'boy," he grumbled. "It's a long trek from

the hotel on the other side of the Nile."
He turned and called to his traveling
companion, his daughter Lady Evelyn
Herbert, who was lagging slightly behind.
"Come along, Evelyn! For goodness' sake,
you're holding us up. Chop chop!"

"I'll take my time, thank you," Evelyn
muttered under her breath. She hitched up
her heavy calf-length skirt a little further
and tottered awkwardly across the
unforgiving valley floor.

"I hope we're going to be back for lunch,
Father," she called sharply. "I simply

cannot stay out in these conditions a moment longer than necessary!"

Carter strode quickly over to the excavation. Carnarvon stopped briefly and ordered the waterboy to attend to the horses. The waterboy grumbled under his breath. He wanted to see what had been found along with everyone else, not look after the horses.

Carnarvon followed Carter down the staircase. Carter was already impatient to proceed and beckoned to the older man urgently. Carnarvon made his way down the rock-strewn steps as fast as he could, but he could not step quickly enough for Carter. When he finally arrived at the foot of the staircase, Carter was eagerly pointing out markings on the plaster wall.

"The design is certainly from the eighteenth **dynasty** of the pharaohs," said Carter in a rush of excitement. "You see the shape of the **cartouches**, the ovals that contain the hieroglyphs? At first, I thought that it might possibly be the tomb of a noble – or perhaps storage for the royal family. Until..."

"Until what?" asked Carnarvon quietly, sitting on the steps and dabbing his brow with a handkerchief. He paused for a moment, suddenly realizing what Carter meant. This was incredible. "So you've found a name?"

A cartouche from the tomb of Ramses II

Lord Carnarvon, Lady Evelyn, and Howard Carter at the entrance to the tomb of Tutankhamen

Lady Evelyn appeared at the top of the steps, trying to brush off the dust caked on her skirt. Then, all at once, she saw the wall marked with ancient writing. As the strangeness of the place enveloped her, she almost forgot about the hot and tiring journey. Almost.

"Did we bring a lunch basket with us?" she called. "We're definitely not going to be back at the hotel in time for lunch, are we?"

Carter paid no attention to what she was saying. He looked at Carnarvon steadily.

"Yes," he said, "we have a name." He carefully dusted off the lower part of the plaster. "Look. The impressions are better preserved down here. Can you see this one? There are nine slaves beneath the picture of a jackal. Here, notice the three sets of symbols spelling out the name of the pharaoh."

Figure of a bird flanked by a cartouche spelling out Tutankhamen

Lord Carnarvon squatted down and peered at the hieroglyphs through squinted eyes. "I can't get close enough, m'boy. This creaky back of mine is acting up. You'll have to translate for me."

Carter pointed to the three sets of symbols, one after the other. "Tut... Ankh... Amen."

Carnarvon fell like a rock back on the steps. He was stunned. He put out a hand to steady himself. "This is staggering," he whispered. "The boy king! This is the tomb you've been searching for all these years. Tutankhamen."

Carter pointed to the top left corner of the plaster. "Unfortunately, it's not all good news. Look up there – can you see?"

There was a triangular section in the corner that looked different. It was smoother, whiter.

"Grave robbers?" asked Carnarvon.

Carter nodded. "I believe it happened in ancient times. If the tomb had been robbed more recently, we would already have found evidence of it. Still, with any luck at all, there may be something left inside. The robbers wouldn't have bothered to reseal a completely empty tomb. What would be the point?"

"Then let's not delay," said Carnarvon, rising to his feet. "Evelyn! Step lively! Let the diggers through!

The plaster seal was demolished. Beyond it was a square-shaped corridor that sloped down and was packed to the roof with chippings of limestone. Carter noticed with growing dismay that a tunnel had obviously been made through the chippings, in the top left corner of the corridor. Clearly, someone had been there before them.

He turned to his men, his face hard with determination. "Let's get it clear!"

For hours they toiled unceasingly. The sun slowly moved across the sky. Long,

jagged shadows moved like broken fingers through the valley, through the thick, dust-filled air. The dusky orange glow of late afternoon softly bathed the steps leading to the tomb.

Up the steps came workers laden with full buckets. Down the steps went workers with empty buckets. It was a steady, unending parade, up and down, down and up. It seemed the work would go on forever.

As the sun began to sink behind the hills, they found the second seal. Exactly like the first, it was a thick plaster block across the corridor.

Carter rushed to examine it. The corridor was long, and what daylight was left could barely reach this far underground.

He pulled a short candle from his pocket, struck a match, and ran the faint glow from the tiny flame across the surface of the plaster. Here were hieroglyphs again, the same as on the first seal, but far better preserved.

Carter's fingers delicately traced the outlines of the hieroglyphs. The light from the candle shuddered, and he realized his hand was shaking. He still couldn't believe it.

*Howard Carter and helpers opening
the tomb of Tutankhamen*

All across the plaster: Tut... Ankh...
Amen... Tut... Ankh... Amen.

Tut... Ankh... Amen... Again, in the top
left corner, there were the telltale signs that
someone, long ago, had dug a hole and
crawled through to the chamber beyond.

"What do you think is behind this wall?"
asked Carnarvon. His voice echoed in the
stone corridor. Lady Evelyn, inching

cautiously along the corridor from the steps, shivered nervously despite the oppressive heat.

Carter shrugged. "Well, we can see that someone has been in here, so it's most likely an empty room. Of course, beyond that there may be additional rooms with a few items deemed unworthy by the robbers. All in all, it's still an important archeological find."

Carter took a trowel from one of the workers and began to dig into the plaster. For several minutes there was only the sound of metal scraping and jabbing at the seal. Carter's face was soon covered with a thin film of sweat and dust. Chunks of plaster dropped to the stone floor of the corridor in swirling gusts of dust. Carnarvon and Lady Evelyn stared nervously at Carter, Carnarvon holding out the candle so that Carter could see what he was doing. Nobody said a word. There were

only the sounds of Carter hard at work,
and an unbearable tension.

Lady Evelyn hardly dared to breathe.
Partly, this was because of the dense,
eye-stinging curtain of dust that hung in
the air. Partly, it was fear of the unknown.
Whether this tomb had been robbed or
not, it was still a tomb. Slow, cold feelings
of dread crept along her spine, just as they
would have done if the group had been
digging up a grave back home in England.

"I'm through!" hissed Carter at last. His
voice sounded loud and thick in the stuffy
atmosphere of the corridor.

Wonderful Things

The candle flickered wildly. Air from inside the tomb streamed out, rushing through the hole Carter had made, like a last gasp that had been held in tightly for thousands of years.

The explorers' lungs filled with the stinking, particle-filled air that had been entombed inside for so many centuries. They coughed hoarsely. Carnarvon doubled over as he tried to catch his breath.

Carter held the candle to the hole to test for poisonous gases. More than once in the past, archeologists and adventurers had been overcome by the foulness of ancient tomb air. If the candle went out, it meant the air in the tomb was no good.

"I think it's safe," he whispered finally. "The chamber can't be filled with rocks, like this corridor was, or the air wouldn't have escaped like that."

"Look inside, m'boy," said Carnarvon. "Can you see if the room is very large?"

Carter moved up close to the hole he had made in the wall. Hot air was still flowing from inside. It brushed against his face. The hole was a ragged, black shape. What was beyond it...?

Carter took the candle. Deftly, slowly, so as not to extinguish the flame, he pushed it through the hole. Grit and plaster fragments edged inside his sleeve as he slid his arm forward.

View of the antechamber with stacked objects and broken items. Had someone been there before?

In the space of a few moments, he was holding the candle up inside the chamber, straining to see into the darkness.

At first, he could see nothing. The glow from the candle was faint and shifting. Then, as his eyes grew accustomed to the gloom, shapes began to emerge.

Animals. Statues. Furniture.

All were reflecting the candlelight with the warm, glowing shine of gold. It was indescribable.

"Carter!" called Carnarvon. "What can you see? What can you see?"

Awe-struck, Carter could hardly speak. "Wonderful things," he whispered quietly. "Wonderful things."

Night had fallen. The workers at the surface were as amazed and delighted as Carter himself as news spread across the valley. It had been an extraordinarily long day, though, and little more could be accomplished until daybreak. Carter knew the excavation of a find as significant as this would take planning, expertise, and equipment. The work would have to proceed flawlessly.

Everyone went home for the night. Carter, Carnarvon, and Lady Evelyn returned to Carter's house at the edge of the Valley of the Kings. He had designed it himself and called it Castle Carter. It was a welcome sight.

Howard Carter's house in Thebes

Despite their exhaustion, none of them anticipated getting any sleep. With their nerves stretched to the breaking point, they discovered a sluggish cobra in Carter's living room, a fresh meal forming a slowly digesting lump in its coiled body. It had eaten Carter's pet bird.

"Filthy beast," growled Carnarvon.

"It's simply doing what it does to survive," responded Carter. "From the look of that snake, my poor bird was ingested about an hour ago."

"That was the moment when we broke into the tomb," said Lady Evelyn. "Father, I'm getting frightened. They say these ancient tombs are cursed. Perhaps we ought to reseal the tomb and go home."

"It's all right," said Carnarvon firmly. Silently, though, he wondered if there might be something to her fear.

"That's all superstitious nonsense," said Carter. "The local people don't believe in all that curse business. It's us Europeans who like to make up silly stories. Our job is to deal in facts, and the facts are that this could be the find of the century."

"I agree," said Carnarvon. "We have to keep our wits about us, for it is imperative that we handle the situation as carefully as possible."

"Something like this can't be kept quiet," nodded Carter. "There has never been a find like it before. It could become headline news around the world, and before we know it, the valley will be swarming with people. We have to get the Egyptian authorities on our side and make sure things are done our way. That means we must figure out exactly what we've got down there – as soon as possible."

"I'll telegraph the museums in London and New York first thing tomorrow," said Carnarvon. "I'll make sure they send out their experts."

Carter paused for a moment. "I was thinking... even sooner than that. In fact, I was thinking we should take a closer look tonight."

"Tonight?" gasped Lady Evelyn. "On our own? In the dark? Down there? You must be crazy!"

"We have flashlights," said Carter. "We have our knowledge of the ancient Egyptians to guide us. What we don't have is time."

CHAPTER

5

A Pair of Eyes

In the dead of night, the valley was cold and still. The heat of the day had vanished completely, and a dry chill had moved in to replace it. Several miles away, the young waterboy had been hunkered down in his bed for hours. He would have kicked himself if he'd known what he was missing.

Down the stone steps of the tomb, along the long echoing corridor, the three explorers carefully crept toward their destination. Each carried a brightly shining flashlight that threw a wide beam across the walls. The sound of their footsteps seemed unbearably loud.

Carter began working to enlarge the hole in the wall. Before long, he'd made a gap large enough for them all to crawl through.

The room was about twenty-six feet wide by thirteen feet deep. Its walls were plain stone. Their feet were the first to touch the chamber's floor in thousands of years, yet there was an oil lamp in one corner and the clear mark of a fingerprint in the paint on a statue. A withered, dry-as-bone garland of

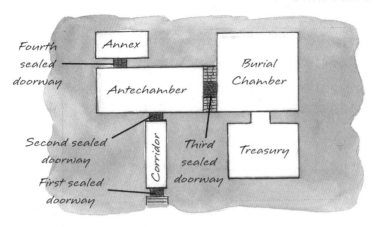

Plan of Tutankhamen's tomb

flowers had been placed in front of the doorway they had just broken through. It was as if the tomb had been sealed only yesterday.

"This isn't right," whispered Lady Evelyn. "I feel like we shouldn't be here."

They aimed their flashlights all around the room, revealing an amazing cache of treasure. There were three gold couches directly in front of them, surrounded by decorated boxes, carved figures, and golden objects of every kind. The horns of a sacred ox sculpture shone out of the darkness.

To the left were the remains of chariots broken by the ancient tomb robbers. In the far corner of the room, beneath one of the couches, was a hole leading into a small **annex** chamber. Carter pointed his flashlight into the tiny room, revealing a chaotic mess of odds and ends.

"The robbers must have come in much the same way we did," said Carter, continuing to shine his flashlight into the annex so the others could look. "Then they stole everything in this annex and left, resealing the entrance. They must have intended to come back, but something stopped them. Perhaps they were killed for the treasures they'd already taken. Perhaps the location of this tomb was lost for some reason. Either way, it's to our great good fortune."

Suddenly, Lady Evelyn gasped. She almost dropped her flashlight in fright.

To the right-hand side of the main chamber was a third seal, blocking off another room. On either side of the seal were tall, black, wooden statues, dressed in gold, facing each other.

"Guardians," whispered Carter.

"What are they guarding?" breathed Lady Evelyn. She shivered deeply.

Between the guardians was a richly decorated box. Carter and Carnarvon lifted it to one side and stood in front of the third seal.

The trio shone their lights around the seal, and the guardians cast eerie shadows on the wall.

Carter began to dig at the base of the seal this time. He placed his flashlight to one side. Progress was painfully slow, and nobody spoke as Carter continued to chip away at the seal.

Once he was through, a fresh pile of rubble had been scattered across the floor. The group remained silent. The carved faces of animals watched from the darkness. The three explorers stood in scant pools of light, hardly daring to move a muscle.

"Well," said Carter, breaking the silence. "Let's see what's inside, shall we?"

The hole was small. Carter shone his flashlight through to the other side. Reflected back were ancient Egyptian designs, gold against a vibrant blue.

"Is it made of gold?" asked Carnarvon, crouching down as far as his weary bones would allow. "What is it? Another wall?"

"No, I believe it's wood," said Carter. "Yes, it appears to be wood with gold laid over the top. It might be a box, or the side of a large ornament."

"Perhaps we should make a second hole to one side," suggested Lady Evelyn. "That way, we could get around it."

Carter lay on his back and pulled himself through the hole up to his shoulders. He coughed as stirred-up dust clung around his face. "I don't think we'll need to," he responded. "There's just enough space to crawl through and stand up in." He struggled to twist himself around. "Whatever this object on the other side of the seal is, it's very big. I can't feel a corner yet."

"You two go through," said Carnarvon. "I'm feeling as ancient as these **artifacts** myself! I don't think I'd quite make the squeeze."

Carter was already hauling himself through the hole into the blackness beyond. He'd left his flashlight in the outer chamber.

The gap between the wall seal and the mystery object was barely two feet. He groped cautiously to the

Bust of Tutankhamen

left. In the pitch black, the tips of his fingers felt the wall to one side, the intricate carved surface to the other. Then he felt something on the floor – something loose and round... Perhaps it was a jar.

He looked over his shoulder. The glow of the flashlights from the outer chamber flickered and shifted as Lady Evelyn crawled through after him.

"Be, careful, Evelyn," called Carnarvon. "Watch your step – don't trip, my dear."

"He still treats me like a child," mumbled Lady Evelyn to herself. After a little struggling, she managed to pull her feet through. She pushed herself up and stood next to Carter. She stretched out her arms. "I can't feel a corner to this object even now," she whispered.

"Neither can I," whispered Carter. "It must be more than fifteen feet wide."

From the outer chamber, Carnarvon pushed two flashlights through the hole. Carter and Lady Evelyn both squinted against the beams of light. Their shadows seemed to ricochet around the room.

On the other side of the wall, Carnarvon sat next to the hole, trying to catch his breath in the stagnant air.

"What is it?" he croaked. He saw the yellowish glowing light through the hole grow dim as Carter swung his flashlight up to take a first look.

"Carter? Evelyn?" he called. "What can you see?"

"Eyes!" called Carter. "An enormous pair of eyes!"

Eyes painted on a wooden sarcophagus

Carter's flashlight shone on the side of the huge object. The light illuminated Egyptian eye designs, placed there to guard against evil. They stared back at him, inches from his nose.

Lady Evelyn had never felt so frightened in her life. She pressed her back to the wall, and held up her flashlight. It lit up the whole room.

The Final Room

The burial chamber they were standing in was similar in size to the first room. While the first room's walls had been bare, the walls in here were decorated with astonishing paintings and hieroglyphs. Their colors were bright and fresh, as if they had been painted only yesterday.

Ancient life and ancient times loomed from the walls, engulfing them in the past. To the right, paintings of twelve monkey gods, representing the twelve hours of the night through which, it was once believed, the sun had to travel so it could shine again the next day.

Above and ahead of them, were remarkable pictures of the boy king, Tutankhamen, and the pharaoh who followed him, Ay. In one picture, Tutankhamen was greeted by the goddess Isis, who was welcoming him into the afterlife. In another, he met Osiris, god of the dead. In another, he faced the dog-headed Anubis, the **embalmer**.

To the left was a scene of the fully mummified king, encased in an elaborate wooden shrine. The shrine was on a barge, being pulled by twelve men in white, wearing sandals on their feet.

The ancient Egyptian depiction of Tutankhamen's funeral ceremony

Lady Evelyn and Carter now understood that the huge object in front of them was that same wooden shrine. It took up almost the entire chamber.

Carter fixed the beam of his flashlight on the strip of floor on which the two of them stood. Objects of various kinds had been placed there, as the ancient Egyptians had left the room for the last time, ready to seal it up. There was a wine jar, as Carter had already found, along with boxes made of reed and papyrus, small **figurines** of Osiris, shriveled-up offerings of food, and much more.

Osiris shown in an ancient Egyptian painting

Yet it was the shrine that commanded their attention. Carter, his eyes wide in astonishment, crept around the edge of the chamber. Every part of the shrine was decorated with carvings and hieroglyphs, and at one end, near where Lady Evelyn stood, was a pair of low doors.

"Lady Evelyn! Come see this – and bring your flashlight!" called Carter. "We'll need more light!"

Lady Evelyn squeezed around the corner of the shrine and crouched down beside Carter. As the beam of her flashlight swung around and lit up the space behind him, she let out a gasp. "What is that?" she demanded.

Carter turned to look. A dark, pointed head with long ears glared out at them from another doorway. This doorway was unsealed. The statue of a jackal was covered in cloth, and it was sitting on a raised platform.

A picture of Anubis, who took the form of a jackal. He guided the dead into the next world and was considered to be the inventor of mummification.

"The final room," breathed Carter. "The treasury. That's the god Anubis, watching over the dead king."

Carter turned back to the small doors in the shrine. In front of the doors, on the floor, had been placed a small perfume vessel on a stand, an offering to

Tutankhamen. The doors were bolted shut and marked with the same cartouche of the jackal and nine slaves that they had seen on the first seal wall, at the foot of the stone steps.

"Is there anything there?" called Carnarvon urgently.

"The shrine is unbroken," replied Carter. "It's complete. It hasn't been opened for more than 3,000 years."

"What's inside this shrine?" asked Lady Evelyn quietly.

"Tutankhamen himself," whispered Carter. "Within this shrine there will be a second shrine, perhaps a third, and inside that, a sarcophagus. Inside that... the mummy of the king. A mummy that has been undisturbed for thousands of years, lying here, in the silence, in the darkness."

With trembling hands, he pulled back the bolt that held the doors shut.

Story Background

Howard Carter's discovery was truly one of the greatest finds in history. Once the tomb itself was discovered, every one of the thousands of objects that it contained was recorded and preserved. Thanks to the discovery, new and important information was uncovered about how the ancient Egyptians lived and died.

    The work of sorting and cataloguing the tomb's contents was long and painstaking. It was a full ten years before it was finished! Incredible treasures were found inside the sarcophagus: the mummy was dressed in intricate jewels and topped with an exquisite mask. It, like many of Carter's finds, is now in the Museum of Antiquities in Cairo, Egypt.